ANCIENT GREECE

Peter Chrisp

Come and explore **MY WORLD** and find out what it's like to live in ancient Greece.

Hello, I'm Cleon

I'm called Crytilla

My name is Hermia

TWO CAN

Created and published by
Two-Can Publishing Ltd
346 Old Street
London EC1V 9NQ

 TM

Editor: Jacqueline McCann
Art direction and design: Helen McDonagh
Consultant: Dominic Themistocleous
Model maker: Melanie Williams
Illustrator: Brigitte McDonald
Photography: John Englefield

First published by Two-Can Publishing Ltd in 1998

Hardback ISBN 1 85434 604 0
Paperback ISBN 1 85434 620 2

Dewey Decimal Classification 938

Hardback 2 4 6 8 10 9 7 5 3 1
Paperback 2 4 6 8 10 9 7 5 3 1

A catalogue record for this book is available from the British Library.

Printed in Hong Kong by Wing King Tong

Some of the words in this book may be difficult to say. Below you will find some ancient Greek words written in **bold**. The words beside them are a guide to help you with pronunciation.

Athene   A-theen-ee
chlamys   clam-iss
Crytilla   Cri-tilla
Delphi   Del-fee
Dionysus   Dy-on-y-sis
Hermes   Her-meez
Hermia   Her-my-a
kerameikos   kera-my-kos
Panathenaia   Pan-ath-en-ay-a
Perseus   Pur-see-us
Piraeus   Py-ray-us
Poseidon   Pos-sy-don
Pnyx   Pe-nix
Thebes   Theebs
Zeus   Ze-yoos

CONTENTS

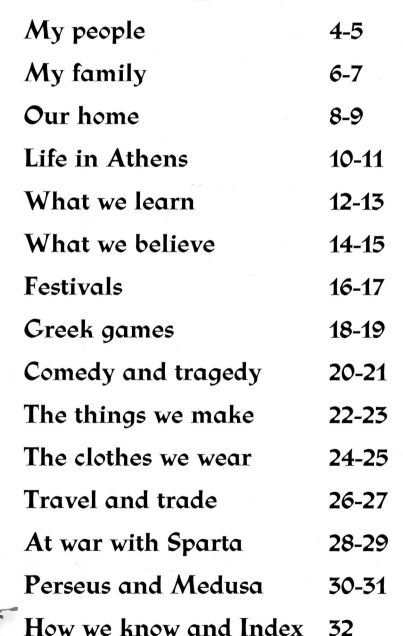

Hello, my name is Cleon. I am nine years old and I come from Athens, a city in Greece. Every city in Greece is independent, which means that each one rules itself. But all Greek people speak the same language and worship the same gods.

Athens, my city

Athens is the richest and most powerful city in Greece. There are many other cities close by, on the islands and around the coast of the Aegean Sea. Each city rules the countryside nearby. Together, a city and the land around it are called a city state. The land around Athens is called Attica.

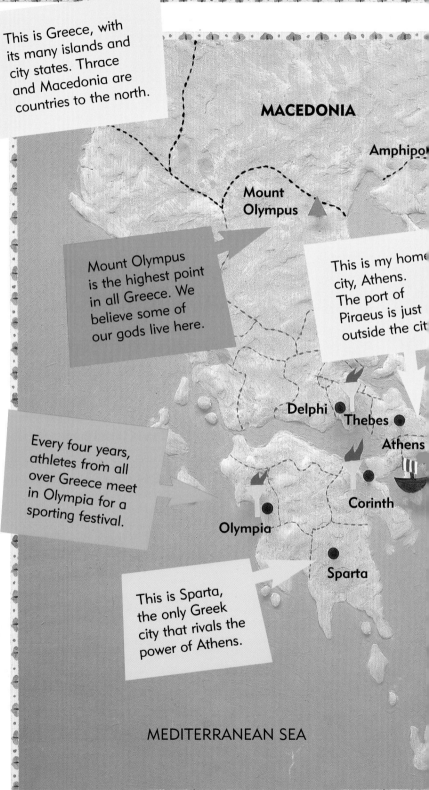

This is Greece, with its many islands and city states. Thrace and Macedonia are countries to the north.

MACEDONIA

Amphipo

Mount Olympus

Mount Olympus is the highest point in all Greece. We believe some of our gods live here.

This is my home city, Athens. The port of Piraeus is just outside the cit

Delphi Thebes

Athens

Every four years, athletes from all over Greece meet in Olympia for a sporting festival.

Corinth

Olympia

Sparta

This is Sparta, the only Greek city that rivals the power of Athens.

MEDITERRANEAN SEA

4

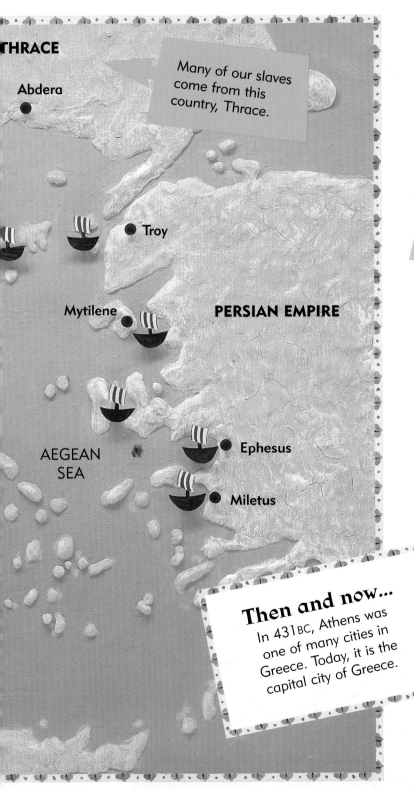

THRACE

Abdera

Many of our slaves come from this country, Thrace.

Troy

Mytilene

PERSIAN EMPIRE

AEGEAN SEA

Ephesus

Miletus

Then and now...
In 431BC, Athens was one of many cities in Greece. Today, it is the capital city of Greece.

Signs on the map

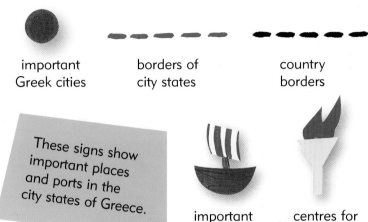

important Greek cities

borders of city states

country borders

These signs show important places and ports in the city states of Greece.

important ports

centres for Greek games

People of Athens

All sorts of people live in Athens. There are foreigners and lots of slaves who have been captured in wars. There are also women and children from Athens. Most important of all are the citizens – free men who are born here in Athens. Citizens hold meetings, make speeches and decide how best to run the city.

Sparta, our rival

Citizens also declare war on other Greek cities. Athens' main rival is a city called Sparta. On land, the Spartans are the best fighters in Greece. But with our great fleet of ships, we Athenians rule the sea. When we go to war, we ask our gods to help us. Most Greeks believe that gods rule our lives and protect us from harm.

5

My family

My father has a workshop where he makes pots. Sometimes, I help him, although he has 20 slaves who work there all the time. We have a slave at home too. Her name is Hermia. She lives with me, my parents, and my sister, Crytilla.

Being a young citizen

Father is a citizen of Athens. On my seventh birthday, I was made a citizen too, although I won't be able to have a say in how the city is run until I'm eighteen. Then, I'll have to serve in the army. For now, though, I go to school, help Father and play sports with friends.

In Athens, lots of boys play hockey. It's important to stay fit because one day we may have to fight for our city.

Spinning and weaving

Like most girls in Athens, Crytilla is learning how to make clothes. It can take many years. First, she has to learn how to spin wool into thread, then how to weave the thread on a loom. By the time Crytilla marries, she will be an expert at making cloth.

Our slave, Hermia

Hermia is a slave-girl who works in the house. She was born in Thrace, a country north of Athens. When Hermia was little, her parents sold her to a slave-trader who brought her to Athens and sold her in the market-place. Hermia missed her family at first, but she's happy with us now.

Crytilla shows Hermia how to weave different patterns into this new wall-hanging.

Hermia has tattoos on her skin, made when she was a little girl in Thrace. Greeks never mark their skin with tattoos!

7

Like most married men, Father spends a lot of his time away from home. Every morning, he goes off to his workshop. Then he passes the afternoon at the market, talking with other citizens. Mother spends her days indoors. She gives orders to the slaves, weaves cloth and organizes our meals.

Hestia is a goddess who protects our family. Before we eat, we throw olives on the fire as an offering to her.

Father's dining room

When Father comes home in the evenings, he entertains his friends in his dining room. Mother, Crytilla and I eat separately. I can't wait to join Father and his friends when I'm older. They listen to musicians playing, and dancing girls entertain them!

At meal times, Father and his friends lie in here on couches. At night, the couches are used as beds.

A statue of the god Hermes stands outside our home. He brings us good luck.

Mother's room

Mother has her own quarters too. When I was little, I spent my time there, watching her dye and weave wool. She has to make robes and cloaks for everyone in the house – even the slaves. There's always lots of work to do.

Mother's weaving room is above the hot kitchen. It overlooks a cool, central courtyard.

Our home is built from mud bricks. Inside, the walls are painted or decorated with wall-hangings.

✴ Serves two people

Let's make an ancient Greek dessert

Find a large carton of plain Greek yoghurt, honey, 50g mixed nuts, plastic bag, string, rolling pin, spoon and bowl.

1 Put the nuts into the plastic bag. Tie the bag with some string. Crush the nuts with the rolling pin.

2 Pour the carton of yoghurt into the bowl.

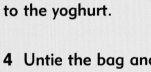

3 Dribble a few tablespoons of honey on to the yoghurt.

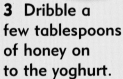

4 Untie the bag and sprinkle the crushed nuts on top.

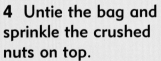

5 Now your delicious dessert is ready to eat!

9

Life in Athens

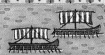

Each city in Greece is run in a different way. In Corinth, only the richest citizens have power, but Athens is a democracy, which means 'the people have power'. At public meetings, all male citizens, rich and poor, decide how to run our city.

This is Athens. The long wall that runs around the outside of the city protects us from our enemies.

Citizens have a duty to attend public meetings. If they don't, slaves may catch them!

I live in the potters' quarter, which is called the kerameikos. It's just inside the city wall.

We call this hill the Pnyx. This is where citizens meet to make important decisions about Athens.

This square is the market-place. Farmers and craftsmen set up stalls here, and citizens meet to talk.

Roping-in citizens

Every ten days, public meetings take place on the Pnyx, overlooking the city. All Athenian citizens are supposed to go, but they don't always want to. If fewer than 5,000 citizens turn up, slaves are sent out to find the missing ones. The slaves carry long ropes soaked in red dye, which stain any clothes they touch. It is a disgrace for a citizen to be seen with red dye on his clothes. Everyone can see that he has shirked his duties!

Meeting at the Pnyx

At the Pnyx, every citizen has the right to make a speech. It may be about changing the law, building a new temple, or whether or not to go to war against Sparta. Afterwards, all the other citizens vote for or against the idea by raising their hands.

Then and now...

Today, in many countries, both men and women have the right to vote and have a say in how their country is run. This is called modern democracy and it is based on old Athenian democracy.

The highest hill in Athens is called the Acropolis. It is a holy place, with marble temples and statues of the gods.

The Parthenon is a new temple dedicated to the goddess Athene.

When there is a play at the theatre, everyone in Athens goes to watch.

Young citizens, like me, go to school. Young Greek girls, like Crytilla, stay at home. I have three different tutors. One teaches me reading and writing, another teaches me music and poetry. My third tutor is a physical trainer.

The gymnasium

The gymnasium is also a place for learning. Thinkers, called philosophers, meet here to talk about life and knowledge. Some philosophers teach us a type of maths called geometry. This is all about measuring shapes such as squares, circles and triangles.

My friend Polus is learning geometry. He says it will help him to build temples when he's older.

My music teacher makes me recite poetry and play my tortoise-shell lyre at the same time!

Physical training

My physical trainer teaches boys how to wrestle, box and run. Sometimes he takes us to a training ground called a gymnasium. Adult citizens go there to exercise, or just to meet their friends and talk.

Preparing for the future

When I'm eighteen, I'll begin my military training and learn how to be a good soldier. All the sport I play now will prepare me for this. Reading books and listening to philosophers will help me to think clearly.

Crytilla's education

By the time Crytilla reaches fourteen, Father will have chosen a husband for her. When Crytilla marries, she'll have to run a house. It will be her duty to make sure that her family and slaves are well-fed and clothed. She will also manage the supplies of grain and wool.

Crytilla has had lots of practice on the abacus. She slides the beads around very quickly!

Keeping accounts

Mother is teaching Crytilla how to keep the accounts for the house. Together, they work out the expenses on an abacus. This is a frame with rows of sliding beads, used for counting.

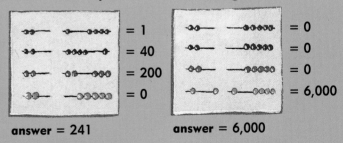

Let's see how an abacus works

On an abacus, the beads in each row are worth a certain amount. Look at the abacus below.

Each bead = 5 → | ← Each bead = 1

Each bead = 50 → | ← Each bead = 10

Each bead = 500 → | ← Each bead = 100

Each bead = 5,000 → | ← Each bead = 1,000

When you count on an abacus, push the beads towards the middle.

Can you see how the beads on the abaci below add up to the numbers given?

= 1
= 40
= 200
= 0

= 0
= 0
= 0
= 6,000

answer = 241

answer = 6,000

Now try to work out the number on the abacus shown right.

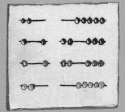

ANSWER 770

13

We believe that our lives are ruled by gods and goddesses. There are many different stories about them. The most powerful god of all is Zeus, lord of thunder. Zeus' brother, Poseidon, rules the sea and the waves. He always carries a special fishing spear called a trident.

Athene's contest with Poseidon

Our city is named after Athene, the goddess of wisdom. Father told me the story of how our city came to belong to her. Long ago, she had a contest with Poseidon on the Acropolis. Each god had to offer the city a gift. The god whose gift was chosen by the people would own the city.

Poseidon carries a three-pronged trident as a sign of his power over the sea.

Let's make Poseidon's trident

Find a broom handle, gold and brown paints, paintbrush, pencil, scissors, thick card and masking tape.

1 Paint your broom handle brown, to look like dark wood.

2 Draw the head of the trident, shown above, on to the card. Now, cut it out.

3 Tape the trident to the broom handle Paint the trident and the tape gold.

Gifts for Athens

Poseidon jabbed a rock with his trident and sea water gushed out. Athene thrust her spear into the soil and the very first olive tree grew there. The people chose Athene's gift because you can eat olives, but you can't drink salt water.

Poseidon and the fleet

Although Poseidon lost the contest, Athenians still worship him. Athens has more warships in its fleet than any other Greek city, and our merchant ships sail safely across the seas. We believe that this is because Poseidon guides our ships and keeps them safe during storms.

Athene is the protector of our city. We believe that when Athens goes to war, she fights alongside our soldiers in battle.

All our coins have a picture of Athene on one side and an owl on the other. The owl is a sign of Athene's wisdom.

Then and now...

An olive tree still grows on the Acropolis in Athens. According to legend, it is planted on the exact spot where Athene touched the soil with her spear.

15

Festivals

Throughout the year, we have many festivals in honour of the gods. My favourite festival celebrates Athene's birthday. It happens every summer and it's called the Panathenaia, or 'all Athens', because everyone in Athens takes part.

Gifts for a goddess

The Panathenaia begins just after sunrise. The people of Athens walk in a long procession up to the Acropolis, where Athene's temple looks out over the city. We bring oxen and other gifts for the goddess.

A wooden statue

On the Acropolis, there is an old statue of Athene made from olive wood. Father says that it dropped out of the sky a long time ago. Like the olive tree, the statue was a gift to the city from our goddess, so it's holy to us.

An ox leads the way through the streets, followed by musicians playing pipes and men carrying olive branches.

I decorated this ox with flowers as a gift for Athene. It's hard work pulling him uphill to the Acropolis!

A new robe for Athene

Once every four years, during the Panathenaia, we make a new yellow robe for the statue. This year, Crytilla helped to weave the cloth. It's a great honour to be chosen to help make the new robe for our goddess.

A ship, carrying Athene's new robe, is rolled all the way up to the Acropolis.

Everyone gathers outside the Parthenon and prays to Athene.

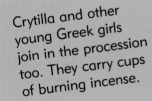

Crytilla and other young Greek girls join in the procession too. They carry cups of burning incense.

Athene's ship

A small ship is pulled through the city. The new robe is fastened to the mast where everyone can see it. Even though it's Athene's birthday, the ship reminds us of Poseidon, who also helped to make Athens a great city.

The festival feast

Outside the temple, oxen are killed and some of the meat is burned for the goddess. The rest is for the people of Athens – it's one of the few times we eat meat. After a huge feast, the celebrations begin, with games, competitions, singing and dancing.

17

During Athene's birthday festival, we honour the goddess with sporting contests. Sport is important to Greek men, and contests are a big part of our holy festivals. We run races and wrestle. I'm sure our gods enjoy watching us!

In the relay race, one athlete runs with a burning torch, then passes the torch to another runner.

The Olympic Games

Every four years, the best athletes from all the Greek cities travel to Olympia for the festival of Zeus, king of the gods. This is the most important sporting festival of all. Every city hopes that its athletes will win at the Olympic Games.

18

Let's make an Olympic torch

Find a dinner plate, pencil, card, scissors, 28cm length of dowel, masking tape, glue, paints and paintbrush.

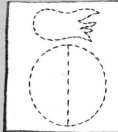

1 Place the plate on the card and draw a circle around it. Cut out the circle. Cut it in half to make 2 semi-circles. Draw a flame shape on the card and cut it out.

2 Wrap a card semi-circle around the dowel. Pull the ends together to make a cone. Tape the ends and glue the cone to the dowel.

3 Paint your torch gold. Then paint the flame fiery colours.

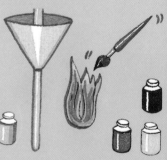

4 Glue your Olympic flame to the top of the dowel, inside the cone. Now you're ready to run an Olympic relay race!

The pentathlon

The most difficult event at the Olympic Games is the pentathlon, or 'five contests'. You have to wrestle, run, jump and throw a discus and a javelin! The winners receive fine jars of olive oil. Sculptors carve statues of some winners, and poets write poems for others.

My father made this olive-oil jar for the winner of the pentathlon. It shows athletes running in a relay race.

This athlete is about to throw a flat, bronze discus as far as he can.

Boxing is a really tough sport! The fight lasts until one boxer gives in or is knocked out.

Then and now...

The Olympic Games are still held every four years with athletes from all over the world taking part. Today, athletes throw the javelin and discus, just as they did in ancient Greece.

In springtime, there's a festival for Dionysus, the god of wine. We hold competitions in his honour, but instead of running races, the people who take part write plays. All the writers hope to win a prize, just like the athletes at Olympia.

Our theatre

The theatre in Athens is enormous. It can seat 14,000 people. Everyone goes – citizens, women, foreigners, children and slaves. The citizens have the best seats. They sit close to the stage.

Only men may act in the theatre. They wear masks to show if they are playing male or female characters.

Sad plays, funny plays

Crytilla likes to watch tragedies. They're serious plays about great heroes and heroines. I prefer funny plays, called comedies, that make fun of well-known Athenians sitting in the audience. Someone wrote about Father at the last festival. He had to pretend that he didn't mind, and laugh with everyone else!

20

Let's make a Greek theatre mask

Find a pencil, stiff white card, scissors, black and red paints, paintbrush, black paper, glue and string.

1 On the card, draw an oval shape the same size as your face. Add holes for your eyes, mouth and nose. Cut out the mask and holes.

2 Paint the areas around the eyes and mouth.

3 For hair, cut lots of long, thin, black paper strips. Roll them around a pencil to make them curl. Glue the ends of the strips to the edge of the mask.

4 Make a hole on both sides of the mask at eye level. Tie a length of string through each hole. Now put on the mask.

In comedies, actors wear padded bellies and behinds. They look really silly!

Then and now...
The Greeks invented theatre and the words 'comedy', 'tragedy' and 'drama'. Today, ancient Greek plays are still performed in theatres around the world.

Athens has the best craftsmen and artists in all Greece. Stone-cutters and bronze-workers make statues of gods and famous people. There are lots of potters too. Most of them live and work in the kerameikos, like my family. Father's pottery workshop is one of the most successful in Athens.

Pictures on pots

Father's slaves make the pots and plates. He paints pictures on them, using a mixture of clay and water. When the pot is baked in the oven, the mixture turns black, while the unpainted parts turn red. Some of Father's pots show the lives of the gods. Others show ordinary things, such as women weaving or boys having lessons.

Hermia is helping me to make a pot. She turns the potter's wheel and I shape the pot as it spins.

22

Let's make a red-figure plate

Find a rolling pin, self-hardening clay, red and black paints, paintbrush, pencil, paper, hole punch, scissors and Plasticine.

1 Roll the clay into a pancake 5mm thick. Curl the edge of the clay upwards to make a slight lip.

2 Leave your plate to dry, then paint it red.

3 Copy an octopus shape on to paper. Cut it out. Now use the hole punch to make holes in the legs. Cut out eyes and a mouth with scissors.

4 Use tiny pieces of Plasticine to stick the octopus to the plate. Paint both the octopus and plate black.

5 Let the paint dry. Peel off the octopus. Your plate is ready to display, but don't eat off it.

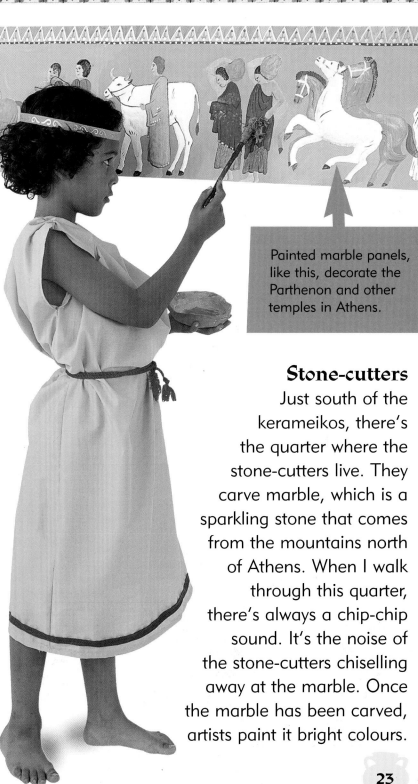

Painted marble panels, like this, decorate the Parthenon and other temples in Athens.

Stone-cutters

Just south of the kerameikos, there's the quarter where the stone-cutters live. They carve marble, which is a sparkling stone that comes from the mountains north of Athens. When I walk through this quarter, there's always a chip-chip sound. It's the noise of the stone-cutters chiselling away at the marble. Once the marble has been carved, artists paint it bright colours.

23

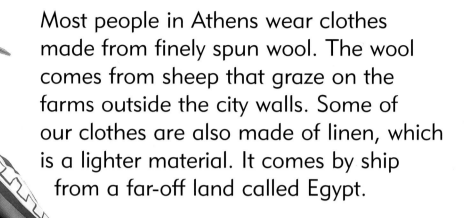

The road to Piraeus is rocky, so I need a sturdy walking stick and thick leather boots.

Most people in Athens wear clothes made from finely spun wool. The wool comes from sheep that graze on the farms outside the city walls. Some of our clothes are also made of linen, which is a lighter material. It comes by ship from a far-off land called Egypt.

Let's make a travel hat

Find a large sheet of red card, pencil, ruler, compass, scissors, glue and masking tape.

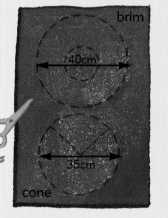

brim

40cm

35cm

cone

1 For the brim, cut a card circle 40cm wide. Cut a circle from the middle, so the brim fits your head. For the cone, cut a circle 35cm wide and remove a section as shown.

Travelling clothes

Today, Father, Crytilla and I are walking down to Piraeus, the port just outside Athens. Father is sending his pots by ship to other Greek cities on the islands. We are all dressed in our travelling clothes. My cloak, called a chlamys, keeps the dust off my tunic. A broad hat protects me from the sun.

Rich and poor

Crytilla wears a red chlamys when she travels. You can tell how wealthy people are by the colour of their clothes. Poor Greeks wear rough, undyed wool, but rich Greeks wear colourful clothes. The most expensive colour is purple because the dye is made from rare shellfish.

Crytilla wears a hat to shade her face. Only poor women who work outside are burned brown by the sun.

2 Make lots of short snips around the curved edge of the cone and bend them upwards.

3 Pull the ends of the cone together so that it fits snugly inside the brim. Glue the ends where they overlap.

4 Slot the cone into the brim, then tape the snips underneath.

Jewellery

Wealthy people also wear fine jewellery. Mother has gold and silver necklaces and earrings that she wears on special occasions. For Athene's birthday festival, Father bought Mother a pair of gold earrings shaped like tiny pigeons.

Greece is a land of mountains and islands. There are few roads, so travel by land is often difficult. Goods are carried over short distances on carts pulled by oxen or mules. For longer distances, it's much easier to go by sea. Most Greek cities are close to the sea.

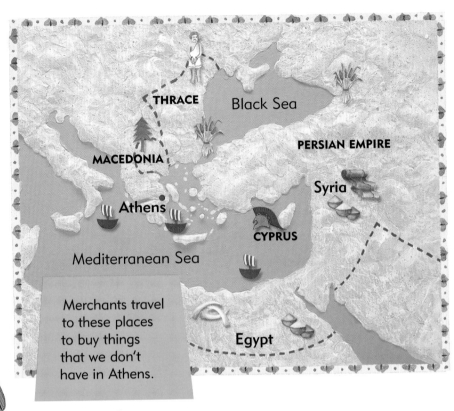

THRACE

Black Sea

MACEDONIA

PERSIAN EMPIRE

Syria

Athens

CYPRUS

Mediterranean Sea

Egypt

Merchants travel to these places to buy things that we don't have in Athens.

Signs on the map

 silk

spices and incense

 slaves

grain

timber

 metal

 ivory

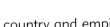 country and empire borders

 These are some of the goods that are shipped to Piraeus and sold in Athens.

Elephant tusks come from Egypt. We use the ivory to make jewellery and to decorate statues of the gods.

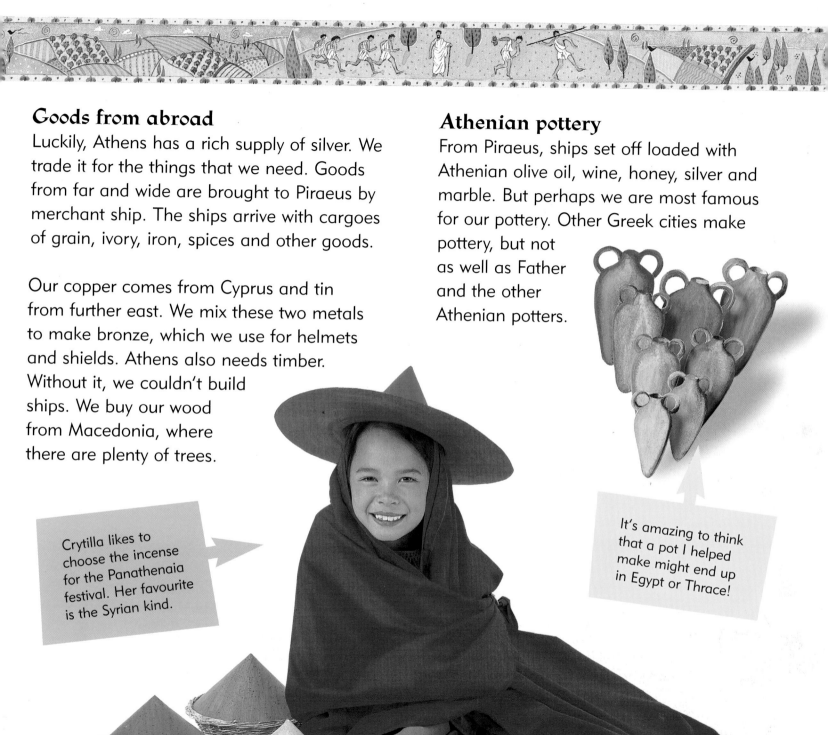

Goods from abroad

Luckily, Athens has a rich supply of silver. We trade it for the things that we need. Goods from far and wide are brought to Piraeus by merchant ship. The ships arrive with cargoes of grain, ivory, iron, spices and other goods.

Our copper comes from Cyprus and tin from further east. We mix these two metals to make bronze, which we use for helmets and shields. Athens also needs timber. Without it, we couldn't build ships. We buy our wood from Macedonia, where there are plenty of trees.

Athenian pottery

From Piraeus, ships set off loaded with Athenian olive oil, wine, honey, silver and marble. But perhaps we are most famous for our pottery. Other Greek cities make pottery, but not as well as Father and the other Athenian potters.

Crytilla likes to choose the incense for the Panathenaia festival. Her favourite is the Syrian kind.

It's amazing to think that a pot I helped make might end up in Egypt or Thrace!

Greek cities often go to war against one another, especially Athens and Sparta. We quarrel for all sorts of reasons. At the moment, the Spartans say that we Athenians are growing too powerful!

Sparta

The Spartans are different from us – they hate comfortable living! Sparta has no fine buildings, theatres, writers or artists. Their men live together in barracks, spending all day practising with their weapons. They can hardly read or write! All they care about is being good soldiers.

Every Greek foot soldier carries a shield. A crab sign in the middle of a shield shows that a soldier is well-armed and protected, just like a real crab!

Let's make a hoplite's shield

Find a large sheet of stiff, white card, pencil, scissors, tape, paints and paintbrush.

1 Draw and cut out a circle of card 65cm wide, and a long card strip.

2 Now choose a symbol for your shield.

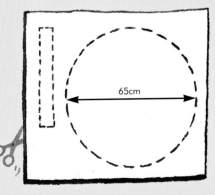

65cm

Citizen soldiers

The Spartans are full-time soldiers, but citizens of Athens fight only during wartime. Athenians have to buy their own equipment too. The richest citizens own horses and fight on horseback. Father is a foot soldier, or hoplite as we call them. Every hoplite must have a shield, a helmet, shin-guards, breast-plate, a sword and a spear.

Our war fleet

The poorest citizens can't afford armour or weapons, so they serve as rowers in our great war fleet, docked at Piraeus. This is one advantage we have over Sparta. Athens is much better at fighting at sea!

All our ships are fitted with pointed battering rams. The aim is to ram an enemy ship and sink it!

A lion shows that a hoplite is strong and fearless. A bear or boar shows these things too.

A bull with a wreath shows that a warrior makes offerings to the gods, and so they are on his side.

The owl is a sign of devotion to Athene. Can you think of a design that says something about you?

3 Paint your shield, then let it dry. Tape the card strip to the back. Leave a loop in the middle so that you can slip your hand through. Now off you go soldier!

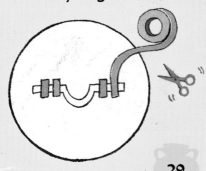

Father often paints scenes from old stories on the vases he makes. My favourite story is about a hero called Perseus, and a frightening monster called Medusa.

The wicked king

Perseus was a fearless young man who lived on an island ruled by a wicked king. Secretly, the king was scared that Perseus would take his kingdom away from him one day. So, he ordered the young man to fetch the head of Medusa. Now Medusa was a frightening woman with snakes instead of hair. It was said that the very sight of her turned people to stone. Brave Perseus agreed to go.

Help from the gods

Luckily for Perseus, the goddess Athene came to see him, with her brother Hermes. Kind Hermes lent Perseus his magic winged sandals, a sharp sword and a pouch. Athene lent him her shiny, bronze shield.

'Whatever you do Perseus,' Athene warned, 'you must not look at Medusa directly. You will be safe only if you look at her reflection in this shield.' Then Athene added, 'First you must find the Grey Women. They are three old sisters who have only one eye between them. Only they know where Medusa lives.'

The Grey Women

Wearing the winged sandals, Perseus flew swiftly to the home of the Grey Women. Patiently he waited until one old woman passed the eye to her sister. Quick as a flash, Perseus snatched the eye. 'Who's stolen our eye?' shrieked the sisters. 'I have!' said Perseus. 'I will return it if you tell me where Medusa lives.'

The Grey Women told him to fly to the end of the earth until he came to a thick forest. There he would find Medusa. Perseus gave back the eye and off he flew.

A deadly meeting

After many weeks of flying, Perseus found Medusa's lair. Bravely, he walked in, never forgetting to use the shiny shield as a mirror. Medusa lay sleeping, but her reflection was a terrifying sight. Her head was a writhing, hissing, mass of snakes!

Perseus crept up on the sleeping monster and with one swishing blow, sliced off her head. Never taking his eyes off the shield, he popped her head into the pouch and set off home.

A gift for the king

When Perseus reached the king's palace, he walked up to the king and, pulling out Medusa's head, said, 'My Lord, I have brought you a gift!'

The king turned and looked at the head of the terrifying woman. Medusa's mouth gaped open and the snakes on her head still hissed and wriggled. In an instant, the king turned to stone, a look of horror frozen on his face forever.

Perseus returned the sandals, sword and pouch to Hermes. Then, he gave the shield to Athene. He also gave her Medusa's head for safe-keeping. Athene placed the head on the goatskin she wears around her shoulders. Next time you look at a picture of Athene, see if you can spot Medusa's head.

How we know

Greek books

Cleon and his family lived over 2,400 years ago, in the year 431BC. This means 431 years 'before Christ was born'. We know about life in ancient Greece because many books have survived. They include speeches made in the law courts, poems about gods and history books.

Pottery

Pots, like those made by Cleon's father, have been found in all the places where the Greeks lived and traded. Pictures on the pots show us how the Greeks dressed and the things that they did every day.

Greek ruins

The ruins of many ancient Greek buildings still stand. Today, the people of Greece are proud of their past and look after their ancient buildings. In Athens, you can still visit the Parthenon and other ancient ruins on the Acropolis.

Ancient Greek plays are still performed in theatres today. From them, we learn about life in Athens and the people who lived there.

Index

The words in **bold** are things that you can make and do.